Promotion
Faster
&
Better

Things you'd do
to get ahead

GYAN SHANKAR

Introduction

If you're ready to take your career to the next level starting from today, keep reading this book as this helps you understand what you need to do, why you need to do it and how you can do it.

Author reveals insider career strategies to get promotion faster & better. Here is a chance to understand the problems and the challenges that you may have been facing and why your current efforts may no longer lead you to your next promotion.

Each chapter is a clear, concise, specific thing to do, to get the promotion you're working hard for. Use them to nail it down, before somebody else does.

Author has provided career management strategies to people who want to move their careers forward faster. He; an ex-corporate HR Head is a consultant & faculty. His books on career, jobs, interviews, management, self-help are live on e-commerce platforms. He holds master's degrees and post-graduate diplomas in management, as well as humanities. He holds the credentials of MBA. PGDBM, PGD-HRD, PGD-TD & MA (double).

Contents

Ch1

Why passed over for promotion?

Most people believe that getting promoted is a reward for past performance. This is absolutely false. Promotions are the ultimate case of "What have you done for me lately?" In fact, employers really don't want to know what you've done, even lately.

They want proof that you can deliver a specific, clearly targeted future. Employers are not rewarding strong performers for their past contributions; they are investing in their future contributions. The sooner you grasp these basics, the closer you will be to getting promoted.

Your past only serves as an indication of what you might do in the future. It is only what you may do in the future that drives the promotion decision. If, you've been working hard and are still waiting to be noticed and rewarded, you may be in for disappointment. No matter what you have done in the past. What bosses care about is what you can do for him or her and the company in your new position.

Top performers are often passed over because of the risk factor. When managers do risk analysis, they must project worst-case scenarios. If the risk is too great, all the benefits in the world will be passed over in favour of a less risky alternative.

The risks associated with promoting you must be manageable and perceived as less horrific than the risks associated with hiring or promoting someone else. A manager who might not at all fear the cost of promoting a man, might raise the risk of promoting, i.e. What is the worst thing that can happen if we promote John? Will he succeed in the new unit? Will his old unit fall apart? Is he gunning for my job? Will he leave the company anyway?

You may be the best person for the job. You have no fatal flaws. You've anticipated and acquired the needed skillset, and you are a well-regarded standout among your peers.
But; if management perceives you as risky, highly talented, diligent, or prone to gaffes, then that perception is your reality. You need to worry about how others perceive you at least as much as you worry about your work.

Whether a promotion involves filling a new position or replacing an existing one, the organization is going to want that job filled on a specific schedule. There may be some flexibility, but if you cannot be extracted from your current duties to achieve a smooth handoff within the window of opportunity, someone else will be getting the new assignment.

Ambitious people tend to get critical assignments. But if having a full plate keeps you from appearing available when a new opportunity arises, you'll be passed over, possibly in favour of some laggard who appears to have plenty of time to take on new duties.

You might get lucky once or twice in a career and have your availability magically coincide with an internal opportunity, but the most successful people systematically make themselves available as opportunities arise. Three factors come into play here. These are:

1. Anticipating the upcoming opportunity.
2. Drawing your work to some kind of closure.
3. Having a replacement ready to take over your old job.

People who manage their careers, as opposed to just experience them, process more information than other people. They see beyond their own tasks and job. They see an intertwined network of internal and external forces working on sectors of the organization. They anticipate senior management moves.

Anticipate change and offer Yourself as the solution. You need to know about internal opportunities before they're posted. Once an opportunity is posted, several things would have already happened. A lot of competition for the opportunity. You have to be demonstrably better than anyone else to get the assignment.

You have to be a change agent having a nose for change, and they place themselves in front of that change, ready to capitalize on it and contribute to the organization's response to that change.

Whether the change is positive or negative is not that important. It's the change itself that creates the opportunity for advantage. For example, if the company is going to move an entire business unit offshore, most of the people in the unit would consider that a disaster. But a true careerist would see it coming opportunity and become the person managing the offshoring process and perhaps even continue as an HQ liaison to that overseas function. They'd take a vacation to go to the offshore country, and they'd start learning the local language.

Introspection of self and awareness of surroundings is a must. Are you avoiding learning something that you need to know to make it to the next level? Has your boss dropped any hints about further training to acquire a new skill? If so, you'd better pay attention. The alternative to advancement is not always stagnation—sometimes it's removal.

You have to be observant. Here are a few examples of observations that, if acted upon, can give you the edge:

• Your competitor is about to launch a product or service similar to the one you've been working on.

• A critical worker is about to retire.

• Your company's revenues have tanked, and budgets are going to be a problem.

• You hear through the grapevine that a coworker interviewed with another company for a job.

• A new manager is coming on board one, two, or even three levels up from you.

• A critical worker one or two steps up from you is pregnant and may be taking maternity leave during a time a critical project is due.

• The company bought a competitor or vendor and needs to integrate or reorganize the acquisition.

• Your boss gripes about a problem, or your boss's boss gripes about a problem.

• The company wants to commercialize a product, enter a new market, start exporting, install CRM, become ISO certified, or the like.

Of course, you should read the internal job postings on your company's intranet every day. But it is anticipating organizational needs that drives a true competitive advantage. Once that posting is public—even internally—you're going to face competition, an existing job description, and managers who have envisioned a solution that may not look like you.

Once you hear about or conceive of a possible opportunity, to position yourself to execute a solution, you will need to establish three things with your boss:

1. You have or can get the needed skills and resources.
2. You are available.
3. Your additional assignment or reassignment.
4. You have the necessary Skills and Resources.
5. Don't overestimate the requirements.

Getting a friend to show you how some software works may enable you to grab an opportunity, while waiting to take a training program may allow the window of opportunity to slam shut.

You should go to training classes and conventions, but the point is, don't delay pitching yourself for an opportunity, because timing is so critical. If you wait to develop deep expertise, you'll be useful to the person who was hired to solve the problem while you were gaining deep expertise.

Some employees who become great implementing someone else's plans. But the people who advance quickly bring ideas and can create plans. So, when you approach a boss about a problem, offer yourself as the solution to that problem.

You have to be available to be considered for promotion! Being available can be crucial. Here is an example. Olivia was up for advancement in the Credit Card department of a large bank. She was a superstar who everyone thought was being groomed to be the future head of that department. But she missed a key promotion because she was put in charge of a headquarters move that made her unavailable for one full year. Right in the middle of that year, her dream assignment came up but was awarded to one of her rivals. During that year, the bank went global, putting its first branches in Columbo. Bank started postings and hiring its first offshore workers, and setting up its first offshore Credit Card function. That was the assignment she missed. A headquarters move is critical. She missed out. You have to be able to draw your work into some kind of closure, and hand it off, to be promoted. If a rival is ready and you're not

Finish Projects. The savvy careerist intentionally finishes projects just as a promotion becomes actionable. He or she will speed up, slow down, hand off, or whatever it takes to make the timing work. Managing time in concert with the needs of the larger organization can make a huge difference in career advancement. You want to be the person senior managers think of automatically when new opportunities come up. You have to be seen as someone who can finish projects. Follow-through, completion, and being ready to pick up the next project—this is the description of you that you want in the minds of the decision makers.

Never be irreplaceable. In order to minimize any problems associated with leaving your old assignment, as well as maximize your attractiveness for the projected new assignment, never be irreplaceable. Irreplaceable people are never promoted. Be a fast -track person. To be a fast-track person you need to make yourself easily replaceable. To accomplish this, you will need to do followings:

1.Document your job.
Documenting your job means that you have written procedures for everything you do, ready and available for your replacement. Policies, procedures, techniques, decision triggers, suppliers, vendors, the secret sauce recipe, all of these can be compiled in binders or intranet files. These, plus the assurance that you will be available to answer questions, can be a one-way ticket to advancement.

2. Train and develop your subordinates.
Cross-train your lateral colleagues to cover your position. Be generous training and developing your staff. As your staff becomes better able to cover for one another, your organizational systems will be more

successful. Relying on structures to get work done is safer than relying on personalities. And anybody who relies on heroes or irreplaceable people is at their mercy.

CEOs spend a lot of their time making presentations, giving speeches, conveying ideas, and arguing against bad thinking in the organization. They are teachers in the truest sense of the word. Teaching, training, developing, guiding, and mentoring your subordinates can be career-advancing practices.

Ch2

Get Noticed

No one has to give you promotion. You have to earn it with your persona and willingness. Focus on deadlines whatever you do. No one cares how hard you work. No one will discover or promote you for being a hard worker. It's up to you (not your manager or your company) to reinvent your job so that you can work where the value is. And when you do that, working gets easier. You suffer less and accomplish more—for your business and your career.

Just because you can work tirelessly doesn't mean you should. It can be really tempting to devote all your time and energy to working, particularly if you are ambitious and competing for a big promotion. But you need to break out of the mode of being overly busy, to give yourself a chance to do the things that are truly necessary to advance. The easiest way to break the cycle is to have something really important competing for your time.

How to get promotion for bigger job with bigger responsibilities and pay check. At the company, you are in charge of business at your place. For change you will be in charge of people. How you work with bosses. How you learn faster and how you handle people. These are parts of your reputation-unwritten parts of resume. No easy task, the promotion. Promotion game requires headwork and friendliness, imagination, planning, skills, tough biasness mind and iron will.

Stay focussed. Don't regret and express even you are sent to unliked location. Listen to people who encourage you, inspire you. Who lives your spirit to be success, inspire you. Who are doing what you want to do next. Stumble happens, that happens to everyone. Fortunately, they are not permanent, you fix them. You overcome them and learn from them. Stumble makes you strong and smarter and make you fearless. Things will flow afterwards. Stay focussed on what you are doing and deadlines. Everyday think you are driving at 200 mile an hour in an international track as trial. You focus only on you run, who is passing, how you are going to take a turn. Can you put a larger radius than that you put last time. That's you are going to get what you want.

The way successful executives get away with not doing everything is by redefining the work as it comes in and negotiating a different, smaller, higher-value set of work.

You need to catch all the work, but not do all the work. As a manager, you are expected to analyse all the tasks that come in, contain them, and propose a plan that will have the biggest impact on the business. You need to choose from all the work you are getting and map out the right work to achieve the right desired business outcomes.

It's your job to realize that and propose it. If you just try and do everything that is asked of you, you fail in two key ways:

1. You can't possibly do it all, so you will fail to deliver some things.

2. But more important, that's the wrong job anyway. If you don't apply strategic thinking and judgment to tune the workload, your boss doesn't need you. She could just as easily assign all the work directly to your team. Your job is to make sense of it and prioritize it correctly and show how a redefined workload delivers the necessary results. This adds real value—and lets you succeed.

Get noticed in your workplace. While working hard is important, your efforts may go unnoticed if you never put yourself in a visible position. If you want to show your employer why you deserve a promotion, you need to be noticed for your contributions to the company. Here are ways to catch your employer's attention:

Look for opportunities where your knowledge and abilities can be showcased, such as staff meetings or performance reviews.

Volunteer to get involved in projects in other departments or participate in company-wide events.

Check in with your employer regularly to find out what they think about your performance, seek advice on how to get promoted or provide suggestions on major projects.

Dress neatly and professionally to make a positive impression on your employer and coworkers.

Demonstrate your leadership skills. As you move to higher positions, you will need to continually improve your leadership skills. The following tips can help you be promoted to a leadership role:

Become a role model for your coworkers and gain their respect through your work performance.

Whenever an opportunity arises, show your supervisor that you can lead and motivate your team members.

Perform exceedingly well in every project, which will make you indispensable to the company and a prime candidate for promotion.

Build on certain qualities that improve your effectiveness as a leader.

Your boss wants you to push back. Your boss is expecting you to think through the business strategy and the workload and offer advice—not to just try and do everything. Your boss needs you to help her with her thinking. You are being paid to judge and decide, not to just do everything you are told.

The people who would come back to you with a thoughtful proposal for what to do and in what order, that would be good for the business, and doable for the team, were the ones who stood out as high performers. The ones who didn't just accept all your ideas and requests, who helped you think through the strategy and priority stood out as high performers. The ones who tried to take on all the work and do everything, resulting in everything slipping, were not so impressive. The ones who simply ignored my inputs, kept their heads down, and did not step up to the strategic thinking and debate were not so impressive either.

There is a tendency to treat all requests from the boss equally. You need to resist this because they don't intend them all equally. They can seem equally excited or serious about a wide range of ideas; some are vitally important; others are just musings. It's hard to tell. They will often forget things they asked for, or change their minds without telling you—you need to check.

Make your boss' job easier. You know what you like. Your boss knows your work. She/he knows where are you. Others are also on hunt. Few are just as smart as you are. They know your past. You have to earn your promotion. Work hard. Keep customers happy. Keep boss happy.

As someone who's been in your role for a little while, you likely know what your supervisor worries about the most. Taking those concerns off their plate can help them see you as dependable and capable. It reinforces that you're a team player and invested in the bigger picture. Try stepping up to cover their responsibilities while they're out-of-office so they can enjoy their time away.

Communicate with your boss. They can help you develop core competencies and keep you in mind when the next promotion arises. You don't have to start the conversation by demanding a promotion. Instead, ask them what it will take to get one. This will put your boss in the position of a guide or a mentor, and get them equally invested in your career success.

Ask how you can improve. You must already be doing an incredible job in your current position to show your superiors that you are capable of handling a promotion. But that doesn't mean there isn't room for improvement. Ask how you can get better. Take time to develop new skills and practice getting feedback like a boss. If you can receive constructive criticism without getting defensive, you'll show that you're ready for the next level.

When discussing or asking for a job promotion, write down and memorize a handful of key points that explain why you deserve it. These might include specific projects or tasks that you went above and beyond to complete on time with stellar results. Understand how your individual work fits into the organization as a whole, and make a case for why you would be the best candidate.

If you've done the work and put in the hours, approach your boss with confidence that you are the right person to be promoted. Your years of experience, work ethic, and knowledge of your organization are valuable assets, and when you have success, so does the company. How to get promoted at work is really just a matter of how you do your job — to the best of your ability and with the desire to get better.

Here's how to advise your executive and negotiate the workload:
 Keep a list of everything your boss asks for.
 Keep a list of the top strategic priorities you are working on.

Have regular meetings with your boss wherever you take out these lists.

Make recommendations about what to prioritize, based on the context of business and the content of these two lists.

When you show your boss these lists, several things happen:

He gets embarrassed, as he hadn't realized he had asked for so many things. When he sees it spelled out right there in front of him, he can see it's unreasonable.

You win lots of credibility for keeping the list, catching everything, and not dropping anything. You make him comfortable that you've got it covered. He trusts you.

You can ask him "Is this still important?" You will find he has forgotten about several of the requests and has decided that others don't matter anymore.

You will realize that you are not beholden to everything on the list!

You will be able to negotiate time lines and suggest priorities.

5 signs you might be getting promoted

So, you've been working hard and getting all the right kinds of attention. You're a team player, your performance reviews are outstanding, and the timing feels right. How do you know if a promotion is headed your way? *Here are 5 signs that you may be getting a promotion:*

1. You're getting more work
Have expectations increased or your role changed recently? While new responsibilities can add more stress, it's a sign that your manager trusts you.

2. You're being asked to train someone
Imitation — or duplication — is the sincerest form of flattery. If you're being asked to train or mentor new employees, it's an endorsement of your skills. It may also be a first step towards handing over your responsibilities to free you up for something else.

3. Your boss asks about your goals
Has your manager started asking you about your long-term career goals? This may be a gentle way of gauging your interest in new opportunities.

4. You're being invested in
Maybe you're being invited to new meetings, or a higher-up takes you out for coffee. If training opportunities or conferences arise, your manager suggests that you should go. Investments of time, resources, and money in your career development aren't made lightly. They are indicators that you're seen as part of the organization's future.

5. You're asked to sit in on interviews
If your manager or HR department asks you to weigh in on new hires, this indicates that they trust your opinion and your understanding of the role.

Ch3

Be Learning

Today, it's extremely unlikely that a person will remain in their first job for their entire careers. According to the U.S. Bureau of Labor Statistics, the average person has 10 jobs by age 40. That number will probably be higher for millennials, many of whom don't plan to stay in their current jobs for more than three years.

In their Harvard Business Review article, 'Are You a Good Boss or a Great One?', Linda Hill and Kent Lineback observe that a lot of bosses fail to fulfil their full potential because they neglect to continue developing their talents. They fail to ask the questions 'How good am I?' and 'Do I need to be better?' Hill and Line back suggest that not enough bosses really know what is needed to be truly effective, or where they want to be in the future.

One of the most crucial qualities employers look for is willingness to learn new skills when hiring new team members. When hiring for senior positions, 34% of companies perceive being a fast learner as the top required skill, and the number rises to 52% for junior roles.When hiring, employers analyse a job candidate's current skills and assess their ability to learn new ones. Growth potential is an essential quality in an employee, and a willingness to learn demonstrates that capability. According to a 2021

Harris Poll survey, this invaluable soft skill tops the priority list for 81% of businesses.

You're a good long-term investment. When hiring a candidate, most businesses assess if they're a current fit and if they'll grow with the company and adapt to emerging changes. Showing that you're constantly developing your skills and acquiring new ones positions you as a worthy long-term investment.

Don't assume the same old techniques will work today as they always have. Don't assume your manager knows all the techniques you should be using to get the results they want. As much as Business Analysis is the same, it is also changing very fast. There are new things to learn at every turn and adapt to keep up in this ever-changing world. Continuous learning and continuous improvement are all that are constant! The context we work in is changing rapidly, which means we need to continue to push ourselves to learn new ways to approach our work.

You keep your skills up to date. Technology and modern work techniques don't stay still, and neither should you. By demonstrating your willingness to upgrade your skills, staying on top of industry trends and continuously enhancing your knowledge, you prove you're a sharp and valuable addition to the team. Keep learning and exploring new techniques and skills related to analysis work. With the explosion of communication tools available today there has never been more for everyone to learn. Job requirements are quickly evolving. To ensure relevance, you need to focus on learning the latest emerging skills. You can do this in a couple of ways.

Set short-term learning goals. If you receive regular performance reviews or feedback, ask your manager which skills they think would help you progress in your role and whether your existing skills need upgrading. A defined date for the next review will provide a clear deadline.

Set long-term development goals. Consider your career goals and identify skills you're lacking to achieve them. For example, if you're interested in advancing to a management position, consider the managerial skills that make your current manager successful, and concentrate on acquiring or improving them. Additionally, actively networking and participating in relevant discussions and events can help broaden your perspective and highlight potential advancement prospects.

Take advantage of company training. Research your company's available training opportunities, and don't hesitate to use them. For example, participate in a workshop on using new equipment, attend a relevant conference, access online training resources or enrol in a sponsored learning course.

Learning should be a lifelong endeavour. People who continually upgrade their skills are not only better employees, but happier and more fulfilled people in general.

When we make time for continuous learning, we are in an act of self-care, taking care of ourselves helps us take care of others. When we have self-care in our lives, we are better team members, bosses, spouses, parents, and friends. Self-care through learning helps us reflect, and challenges us to think outside our current paradigms of how we relate to others and process information. This can have a huge impact on our outlook, mindset, and approach to various problems we are working on solving. No matter your age or experience level, learning and a "growth mindset" can set you up for less stress and better wellbeing.

It must be human nature to shy away from tasks that are difficult. We may wish to feel safe, in a zone where we know exactly what to do to get to the right answer. The problem with staying in a safe zone is that little if any learning will take place. In order to expand our learning, we have to expand our horizons and engage with interesting and tough problems in a way that challenges us. We must realize that not all difficulties are a bad thing.

It crucial to demonstrate your willingness to learn? When a job candidate shows that they're open to changing, learning and upgrading their skills, they instantly become a better investment. When navigating your career path, demonstrate your willingness to learn so employers can see your growth potential.

Demonstrating your willingness to acquire new skills, stay on top of industry trends, and continuously improve your performance and knowledge is instrumental to career success. It can help position you as a valuable addition to the team, a smart long-term investment for the company, and a worthy candidate for promotion. Additionally, actively seeking out avenues for improvement will help open new career paths, keep you sharp, increase your work-life satisfaction and ensure you make the most of any emerging opportunities.

Demonstrate your willingness to learn and grow

Indicating that you're eager and quick to pick up new skills and techniques will speak in your favour when it comes to hiring or getting a promotion. There are many ways to show an employer you're willing and eager to learn new skills. Here are five suggestions from experts to get you started.

1. Provide examples of how you are self-teaching.
The advice to be a lifelong learner may seem like a cliche, but demonstrating that you are an active learner can play a significant role in a hiring manager's decision. In a past or present position, how did you volunteer for a stretch assignment and achieve great results by pushing yourself to learn a new skill or strategy? If you're interested in pursuing certifications to show you're an active learner, consider cybersecurity certifications, CRM certifications, IT certifications and sales certifications.

2. Highlight your dedication to growth.

When speaking about previous work or volunteer experience, highlight your participation and what you learned to show your growth. Receiving a quick promotion in a previous company can speak volumes. Even a minor title bump demonstrates your ability to adapt quickly and take on new tasks. Employers love to see what you're actively participating in to get you to where you want to be." "Maybe that's a side hustle that creates extra practice in your skill set, or maybe that's participation in webinars and community meetups. Show your participation and enthusiasm beyond just your roles.

3. Embrace emerging technology.

Since many industries center on technology, an essential part of modern-day growth is embracing new technology as it comes out. Embracing new technology is especially important if you're pursuing a career in the tech industry. In addition to reading about new technology, tech-focused job seekers can benefit from participating in supplemental courses and certifications to receive hands-on experience. A hands-on approach to new technology shows employers you're willing and able to learn.

4. Explain how your ideas have helped the bottom line.

It's not enough to be dedicated to learning. Consider how your willingness to learn benefited your assignments. Identify what you need to learn. Reflect and identify any tasks you might be avoiding or struggling with during the workday due to a lack of relevant knowledge or skills. This can help you zoom in on areas that need improvement. If your responsibilities have increased over time, consider if you've had sufficient training to succeed. Outline the skills you lack or need to upgrade and consider requesting support to improve your knowledge.

How to make learning a habit

Any time you find yourself getting too comfortable with your format of learning, it's a good idea to change something that makes the learning more challenging for you. This is the kind of difficulty that is desirable and will help you meet your learning goals. Take advantage of the, you need to be constantly learning. And that means making lifelong learning a habit. Here are four tips to help you make learning a habit:

1. Set aside time each day for learning. Set aside some time each day even just 30 minutes to read, listen to podcasts, or take an online course. By making time for learning each day, you'll be more likely to stick with it and make it a habit.

2. Find a learning method that works for you. Some people learn best by reading, while others learn better by listening to audio or watching videos. Find a learning method that works best for you and stick with it.

3. Take advantage of free resources. There are many free resources available online, including podcasts, e-books, and online courses. Take advantage of these free resources to help you learn new things.

4. Be patient and persistent. Learning takes time and it won't happen overnight. Be patient and persistent in your efforts and you will eventually see results.

Ch 4

Master the Sales Skills

When IBM ran into financial trouble the early 1990s, the company brought in a new president, Lou Gerstner. He immediately called in his friends from McKinsey & Company, one of the largest and most respected management consultancies in the world. He asked them to use their investigative skills to determine why IBM sales, market share, and profits were falling. They immediately went to work. In less than six months, the consultants were back. They assembled the senior executives and told them, "*We have found your problem.*" They asked, "*What is it?*" The McKinsey consultants replied, "low sales." The executives agreed that this was the problem and then asked, "*What is the solution?*" The McKinsey consultants said simply, "*High sales.*" "Again, the senior IBM executives pointed out that these two answers were obvious. But how would these high sales be achieved? At the end of this study, the McKinsey people explained their most important finding: In a sales-driven organization, the sales manager is the pivotal skill. Nothing will bring about faster and more predictable increases in sales performance and sales results than training sales managers to do their job more effectively. As a sales manager, you are the most important person in the sales-driven organization. You have more influence on the level of sales and, ultimately, the level of profitability of the company than almost any other person. You are vital to the success of the company.

The sales manager is one of the most valuable and often one of the least appreciated executives in the company. It is the sales manager who sets the standards and quotas for the salespeople and sees that they achieve them. The development of excellent sales managers is an essential requirement for all successful business enterprises.

Sales management is an inexact science because salespeople are very different from most other employees. A sales manager must be a friend, a counsellor, a confidant, a stern taskmaster, and an efficient business-oriented executive, all at the same time. Salespeople have emotional highs and lows, selling booms and slumps, and a variety of eccentricities that require a person with tremendous patience and superior human relations skills to manage and control them. The superior sales manager is a person who can meld a variety of different personalities into an effective sales team that can produce predictable and consistent sales results, month after month. Persistent application of the principles taught in this book will allow a sales manager such as yourself to achieve better sales results—starting immediately.

The sales profession has changed dramatically in the last few years. The Internet has made product knowledge a commodity, and the old sales approach of feature-advantage-benefit selling doesn't work with today's savvy, well-educated prospects. So, what's a salesperson to do? How do you win business in this new buying environment? Top sales professionals recognize today's changing business environment and are equipping themselves with emotional intelligence skills.

Emotional intelligence and understanding the what, why, and how of emotions is best discovered through self-awareness and self-discovery. In simple terms, emotional intelligence (EI) is the ability to recognize your emotions, and to correctly identify the emotion you're feeling and know why you're feeling it. It's the skill of understanding what trigger or event is causing the emotion and the impact of that emotion on yourself and others; and then adjusting your emotional response to the trigger or event in order to achieve the best outcomes.

Millions of dollars are invested in sales training every year but it often doesn't produce the desired revenue or changes.
A common hot button for salespeople is when a prospect begins to question them about the value of their product or service. "Why are you so high? Your competitor is half your price." If you don't recognize this hot button, your emotional response can be to quickly concede and offer a discount.

The emotionally intelligent salesperson recognizes the potential hot button, manages his emotion, and changes his reaction. The response is calm and smart: "The reason our services are on the high end of the investment is because many clients, prior to working with us, had purchased on price. As a result, the purchase ended up costing more because they could never get a live body on the phone for problems. This led to missed deadlines, which affected their reputation and repeat business from clients."

Many sales managers make a common mistake of hiring new salespeople based primarily on the number of years in sales or industry experience. This isn't necessarily bad. However, there's a lack of focus on integrating soft skills into their selection process. More than 90 percent of the reasons for a bad hire consistently relate to soft skills. We hear responses like, "He couldn't get along with other departments," "She had a bad attitude," and "He couldn't read people very well." Notice that none of the responses are linked to the hard skills of selling, such as "He just couldn't close," "She didn't meet with the right decision makers," and "He wasn't good at selling value."

The Role of the Sales Manager

Top role of the sales manager is to generate the sales that are essential to the survival of the company. The sales manager achieves these sales results by working with and through other salespeople. One of your most important jobs is to determine the level of sales you want to achieve daily, weekly, monthly, quarterly, and annually. Establish these goals as your targets and then work back to the present day. Decide what you will have to do to hit those targets in those time spans. To hit your sales quotas, you will have to plan, project, and organize people, resources, budgets, and promotional materials. You must determine the plans of action that you will follow to get from where you are to where you want to go in terms of sales results. The better planner you are, the more successful you will be, irrespective of what is going on in the marketplace. Another major responsibility you have is to communicate and motivate. You get your work done through other people. Their results are your results. You need to be able to give your people the information, resources, and incentives they need to get their jobs done. Your next key function is to measure results. One of the most important business principles is this: "What gets measured gets done." If you can't measure it, you can't manage it. If you don't measure it, it's probably not going to get done at all. That's why you need clear objectives, standards of performance, and assigned responsibilities for every person.

The two primary activities of a sales manager are first, to create value, and second, to generate revenues. You should spend 80 percent of your time creating value and generating revenue, all day long. Almost everything else you do, including and especially dealing with email, social media, messages, and phone calls, are diversions or distractions taking you away from creating value and generating revenue. In the final analysis, your ability to get sales results will be the single most important determinant of your success.

All sales work is done by teams. Your job is essentially that of a team builder and a team leader. All teams depend on the peak performance of each team member. Your job is to assemble a superior team first, then to bring every member on the team up to top performance. Your goal is to build the best sales organization you can and to win in competitive markets.

Top salesmteams exhibit six key winning characteristics.

1. Coaching & Leadership
But for a crack sales team to perform well, everyone has to know who the coach is. As the sales manager, you are the one in charge. You are the person who sets the standards and calls the plays.

2. Commitment to excellence
Vince Lombardi said, "Winning is not everything, but wanting to win is." Perhaps the best motivator of all, in sales or in sports, is the desire and determination to "be the best." Unfortunately, if you do not make a clear spoken commitment to be the best with your salespeople and your team, you will unwittingly slip down into mediocrity.

3.Open Communication

In top sports teams, there are no games and no politics among the players. Everybody tells everyone else what they think, all the time. There are no secrets, no sulking, and no hidden agendas. Psychologically, to perform at their best, people need to be able to talk to their bosses, to ask questions, and to get feedback. Top players need to feel that they can express their concerns to their managers without fear of disapproval or criticism.

4. People Development

Top teams focus intensely on training their players continually, day in and day out What top companies and top sales managers have discovered is that the return on investment (ROI) from sales training is ten, twenty, and thirty times greater than the amount they invest. The more money they pour into sales training, the higher their sales and profitability.

5. Selective assignments

On excellent teams, people are assigned to a position where they can make the greatest contribution to the overall success of the team, based on their special talents and abilities. In sales management, some of your people will be best at selling one product or service and some will do better with other products or services.

6. Strategy & Planning

One of the most important things that you can do, and that nobody else can do, is to plan for the activities and sales results of your team. Sit down each day and think about what you could change, improve, or do differently. What have you learned recently, and what actions could you take to improve individual or team performance? To quote Vince Lombardi again, "To build a championship team, you must become brilliant on the basics."

Ch5

Ways to Show Your Boss You are Ready for Promotion

1. Make Your Boss Obsolete

It's ironic, but the best way to get promoted is to make your boss' job easier. And the best way to do that is to make his or her job obsolete. You're not really putting your manager out of a job—you're allowing him or her to trust your work. In turn, he or she can focus on new areas that the higher-ups have needed to address for some time. Strong work goes up the chain, improves the company, and gets you noticed.

2. Summarize Work Visually

When talking about your work, give us something to look at. When you answer the question, 'Why are people buying?' show a chart of the top responses as well as how many people gave each response. It makes everyone a believer when we can see a quick visual snapshot that backs up what you're saying.

3. Own Projects from Start to Finish

Organizations place a premium on individuals who follow through on tasks. If you can prove that you can consistently own projects from start to finish, you will not only get promoted, but you'll also make yourself indispensable.

4. Keep a Positive Attitude

The people who typically get promoted keep their cool under stress. They also act as a role model to everyone around them. They meet deadlines and ask relevant, intelligent questions that help clients be happier with our services. When an issue arises, they want to solve it and work to avoid future problems by learning from their mistakes.

5. Raise Other Team Members' Performance

I look for people who are completing their assignments and asking what that next task is going to be. They help their colleagues instead of stepping on them in their climb up the ladder. I love to promote people on my team who raise the performance of everybody around them.

6. Make Your Boss Aware You Want the Promotion

It seems quite simple, but expressing your desire for a particular promotion is very helpful. Sometimes management may not know you want it, or has not thought of you as a candidate, especially if it's outside of your current department. Often management will tell you what you need to do to get the position if they know you want it. Be humble, inquisitive, passionate, and hungry.

7. Show Pride in Your Work

Competence, diligence, intelligence, loyalty—these all matter, but what matters most is the inherent will to do the best work possible. The work is what matters, and employees who take it personally, who own their work as a reflection of their values and take pride in doing good work, are the employees I trust with positions of responsibility.

8. Avoid Office Politics and Gossip

The qualities we considered most were those that demonstrate integrity and trustworthiness—which we measured by looking at who chose not to participate in office politics and gossip. While it's important to understand the balance of office politics, individuals who are able to rise above the temptations stand out most as those I think would be the fairest to others in management roles.

9. Display Commitment

When people are really committed, you can tell by the quality of their work, the effort they put in, and the relationships they develop. When employees show commitment, we notice and try to reward them with deserved promotions.

10. Demonstrate That You Can Solve Client Problems

To get promoted, you have to show that you can take the initiative and help our clients solve their problems.

Since I run a marketing company, I am looking for people who can implement creative and effective campaigns that make both us and our clients shine. This also means being able to work independently, without having to be told what to do every step of the way.

11. Be Exceptional

I want to promote from within, but it's important that clients and co-workers see the justification. I need team members to make a significant impact on their clients—who really wow them. If they don't have a client-facing position, they should be the go-to person for their colleagues.

12. Make Money

If someone is making money, they'll be promoted. Making money is the ultimate internal currency. All other internal performance metrics can be translated into the money-making metric. And yes, saving money is making money, too. Anyone who understands enough of the business ROI levers to structure and ask for more resources or a different title will probably get it and keep moving up each time the argument is made.

13. Attract and Manage Great Talent

At a fast-growing company, hiring quality people quickly is one of the most important goals. That's why

I place great value on people who can bring in additional talent through their existing networks, convince that talent to join our company, and cultivate those individuals into productive team members. Showing that you can build and manage a profitable team is a clear path to promotion.

How to Ask Your Boss for a Promotion

The single-biggest mistake people make looking for a promotion is they think if they keep their head down and work hard, they'll get one. That's giving away your power. Instead, be proactive – if you believe you are worthy of a promotion or would like to earn one down the road, ask your boss for it. How? Here are a few best practices:

1. Ask your boss what it'll take to get a promotion, instead of demanding one that moment. Unless you are truly willing to follow through, it's not a good idea to give your boss an ultimatum like, "Give me a promotion or I'll quit." Instead, you should tell your boss with what you want early in your relationship with them and work with them to make it happen. If you want to be promoted, tell your boss that and ask them what it'll take. This will also give you a realistic timetable and guide to getting that promotion. This will also turn your boss into your biggest cheerleader, instead of a potential adversary.

2. You have a business case ready for why you should be promoted. If you followed step one, when you officially ask your boss for a promotion shouldn't come

as a surprise. But still, regardless of how good of a relationship you have with your boss or what you've agreed upon with them before, many times you'll still need to make the business case on why you should be promoted.

3. There are several mistakes' people make when asking for a promotion that'll hurt your chances. Avoid the followings:

Don't compare yourself to others. Don't tell your boss that you should be promoted because your colleague – who does half the work you do, mind you – just did. This can make you come across as unprofessional and criticizes both the person who was promoted and the people who agreed to promote him or her.

Don't think a good personal relationship with your boss will lead to a promotion. It helps to have a good personal relationship with your boss, sure. But that alone won't mean a promotion – your boss needs to justify to their boss that you are worthy of promotion, and them saying "I like this person" isn't going to cut it.

Know the state of the business. The worst time to ask your boss for a promotion is after a layoff – you better have a really, really compelling business case. Know the state of the business – along with being a key quality to getting promoted, it'll help you frame your business case.

Getting emotional if your boss doesn't promote you. If you believe you deserve a promotion and you don't get one, you might get emotional. That's fine – if you do it alone. But don't get emotional toward your boss. It could ruin your relationship with them and paint you as unprofessional.

One of the best ways to prove to your organization you are worthy of a promotion is committing to learning new skills. This shows that even if you don't have the skills needed to do a bigger job yet, you could learn them. So, really, learning any new skills relevant to your job is a major plus

The Qualities You Need to Exhibit to be Promoted

Promotions aren't just handed out because you want them. You need to earn your promotion by first acting in a way that's promotable. Here are the qualities you need to display to be seriously considered for a promotion:

1. You need to be good at your job.
This sounds obvious. But, if you aren't performing above-average in your job, it's nearly impossible to be promoted.
So, put your focus here first. But being good at your job isn't enough – being good at your job just proves that you are good at your current job. To be promoted,

you need to prove that you'd be good at a bigger job. The rest of the qualities demonstrate that.

2. You prove you can develop yourself.
This is the difference between a high-performing employee who will stay in their role forever and a high-potential employee who will quickly move up the ladder. A high-performing employee will do their job well, yes. But their performance reviews will look the same year-after-year – the same portfolio of strengths and weaknesses. Conversely, the high-potential employee proves to their employer that they are not just going to excel in the role they have, but push themselves to continually improve. This means they take on new and different responsibilities. It means they are aren't afraid of lateral moves, if it means the chance to master new skills. It means they actively solicit feedback from others to understand what they are weak in. And, it means they learn on their own time.
If you do those things, it'll show that you have a growth mindset, not a fixed one. And that's how you become seen as a high-potential employee, instead of just a high-performing one.

3. You are easy to work with and have strong relationships across the organization.
Being promoted isn't a decision your boss makes in a vacuum. At most organizations, promotions require the green-light of other people within your organization as well. And there's no quicker way to hurt your chances of getting promoted than making

enemies. Instead, you want to do the exact opposite – you want people to be on your side, to root for you to get promoted.

How? Be a good partner. Treat people with respect, even if they don't treat you with respect. Be aware how you show up. It might feel good in the moment to get frustrated at someone or blow someone off, but that can kill your chances to move up within an organization.

4. You see the bigger picture.
Being promoted means getting a bigger role within the organization. And the best way to show that you are worthy of that bigger role is by seeing beyond your day-to-day and thinking strategically about how your efforts can most help the organization. This means really understanding the business you are in and how your role – and your department – fits in. That'll empower you to make more strategic suggestions to your manager. It also means understanding the culture your organization is looking to build and acting in a way that exemplifies it.

5. You are a "yes" person.
This doesn't mean you should agree with everything your boss says – in fact, disagreeing thoughtfully will help your career. It's good saying "yes" when there are opportunities to expand your role. Maybe there's a group you can join within the office. Or a pilot you can be a part of. Or a new, lean team that needs members.

Whenever possible, say yes if it means an expanded scope.

Obviously, you need to prioritize smartly here. But, if you can start taking on new responsibilities and projects outside your core role, you prove to your boss that can handle a bigger job – while also building relationships with more people across the organization.

6. You listen.

There's this misconception that you need to dominate every conversation you are in to prove to everyone you are indeed a leader. In reality, the exact opposite is true. One of the best ways to improve yourself, to form great relationships with others and to become more strategic is to actively listen. If this isn't a strength of yours, make it one – this course can help.

7. You are purposeful with what you say and how you say it.

"Language is everything. Your words tell people who you are – your language is imperative in your ability to get promoted."

Tips to enhance your promotability

1. Learning to Be Promotable. To land a promotion, you need to do more than just excel at your current job. You need to have the right skills, say the right things to the right people, and demonstrate your ability to lead.

2. Having an Honest Career Conversation with Your Boss. To get what you want, you need to ask. Dialog is what opens doors. If you're at the place in your career where you need to have a truthful conversation about what comes next.

3. Developing Executive Presence & Strategic Thinking Learn to project self-confidence, clarity, and credibility even under conditions of stress, pressure, and uncertainty. Strategic thinking is the ability to think on a big and small scale, long and short term, and into the past and the present. While strategic thinking is a valuable skill for everyone in an organization, it becomes increasingly essential as you ascend the ladder. In fact, you may have a difficult time being promoted or succeeding as a leader without it. Yet, no one formally teaches strategic thinking— so it's critical to take the initiative and learn how to do it yourself. This course teaches managers and leaders how to use strategic thinking to guide the direction of their teams and come up with solutions to key business problems. Carve out time to think about strategy, gather data, learn from the past, create a vision for the future, and implement strategic thinking within your team.

Make sure your manager's peers know how hard you work and how much you care about the company. If your boss isn't giving you opportunities to demonstrate that to others, you'll need to do it by slowly building your own relationships with people in a position of influence, says leadership professor Herminia Ibarra. Start by getting to know a couple of people outside your immediate group. The relationships can be casual—based initially on chitchat about movies or hobbies—or you can ask for formal introductions.

Ch6

Make Feel Good
The Boss Who Holds You Back

The ultimate organizational fact of life is this that the person with the most power wins. Most of the time, the person directly above you in the hierarchy has more power than you do. Your boss can affect your pay, your reputation, your assignments, your advancement, and the general quality of your life. Once you accept this fact, what naturally follows is the need to effectively manage your boss. We usually think of this the other way around: your boss is responsible for managing you and should therefore treat you with respect, courtesy, and—I'll say more about this one in a minute—fairness.

Bosses are tricky. You know this, because you have one yourself. But what if you're stuck working for a boss who's particularly difficult? There's no easy answer to this question, but there are some basic guidelines that may help you on your way.

First and foremost, remember that they're not here just to be difficult — they're human too! Keep in mind that their motives may not be malicious or sinister; the point of being a boss is to be in charge and take on responsibility for the things happening around them. If it turns out that you found it impossible to keep these things in mind when dealing with your own boss, it might be time for a change of work environment.

An executive narrated, "number of years ago, I went sailing with my boss at the time, and it started out wonderfully. The sun was shining, the wind was steady, the sea was calm. Best of all, my manager was in a great mood, and we were having a great time talking about work issues as well as other matters. A few hours later, though, a front moved in and the sea became rough. As conditions deteriorated, he reverted to form. As a manager, he was a Bully type— tough, aggressive, decisive, used to giving orders and having them obeyed without question. Though he could be gracious and accommodating when it suited his purposes, his classic Bully traits would come to the surface whenever he was under significant stress. As the wind stretched the sails tight and the boat rose, fell, and tilted at a precarious angle, my boss ordered me to put my life jacket on. He snapped at me when I asked a question. He shouted at me to get something from the other end of the boat and told me, "Hurry up!"

"How can I deal with my boss?" It is a question employees ask not only when they are frustrated by someone who they view as a "bad" boss, but when they are trying to help a "good" boss do the right thing.

Most bosses today work in highly stressful environments. Every manager is trying to navigate through stormy seas as companies and industries undergo significant change. To deal effectively with a boss under pressure, you need to know he or her well. This does not mean you need to know boss's personality as much as her managerial persona. Certainly, the two concepts are related; many people's best and worst qualities are muted when you're having lunch with them or interacting with them socially, but when they put on their boss hat and they're struggling to meet a tight deadline, they change. They exhibit certain traits that define them as bosses rather than as people.

You can manage them if you possessed a number of strategies for a number of different boss types. It will be useful if you start thinking about following types of bosses

• The Bully—aggressive, command-and-control type; can deliver great results, but can also take bad risks and be a tough person to work for.

• The Good—consistent, calm, communicative, but has problem with risk or anything that upsets the applecart.

• The Kaleidoscope—shifting persona focused on accumulating and consolidating power; extremely bright and business savvy, but also difficult to get to know the real person and easy to resent controlling personality.

• The Star—high-energy, dramatic, and action-oriented, but has little patience with red tape or anything that requires patience; impulsiveness can get the group in trouble.

• The Scientist—highly logical and reliant on a theory of the case, open to feedback, but also can stubbornly stick to a theory beyond all reason; can also be distracted and difficult to communicate with in this state.

• The Navel—big ego in need of constant feeding; this ego can drive group to decide and execute with speed and skill; can also drive people to distraction as this boss makes everything about him.

What makes your boss tick?

If you can answer this question, you have a much better chance of managing your manager.

First, you often don't stay with one boss long enough to figure him out. The turnover in organizations is so high that either your boss leaves or you do before you've had the time to get to know him well. You can't size up your boss in one or two or even three meetings. It takes a series of interactions in a variety of situations before you can start determining your boss's makeup. If your boss is around for only six months, by the time you start getting a handle on who she is, she's gone.

Second, increased travel and flexible work schedules often make it difficult to get to know a boss, even one who is there for a sustained period of time. You may be on the road a lot, as is your boss, so your face-to-face interactions are infrequent. Similarly, you may be working out of your home while he's in the office (or vice versa); you may be located in two different offices; or you may be working different schedules.

Third, so much of our communication with our colleagues these days is via electronics—phones, e-mails, teleconferences, text messaging, and so on. If this is the main way you get to know your boss, you probably don't know him well at all.

Fourth, you may be splitting your time between two or more bosses. For instance, you're a member of a functional group with one boss and a member of a cross-functional team with another boss. This dilutes time spent with a single boss and makes it harder to figure her out.

Given all this, you need to ask yourself a series of questions about your boss to figure out what makes him/her tick. The following general ones will get you thinking in a "ticking" frame of mind. This is not a definitive list of questions by any means. You probably can (and should) create some of your own.

• What single behaviours or attitude is most likely to upset your boss?

• When is your boss most pleased with direct reports? What do they say or do during the course of carrying out assignments or in meetings that earns his approval? What are your boss's demons? What work issue do you think keeps him up at night pacing the floor?

• What do you think your manager's career objectives are? What capstone position is he aiming for? What does he need to accomplish to achieve these objectives?

• What drives your manager? What noncareer motivators push her? Is she after power, money, fame, security, knowledge, innovation, etc.?

• What trait or attitude that you possess makes you think you are well-suited to work for this particular boss? What trait or attitudes makes you think you are ill-suited?

- If your boss were a famous movie star, politician, or other celebrity, who would he be? What particular traits does he share in common with this well-known individual?

Turn bad boss situations into good & great ones

Successful have demonstrated that they do it by taking charge of managing the relationship, resulting in three types of benefits:

Facilitating the day-to-day personal interactions between you and your boss. Is there a lot of tension between you and your boss that makes you uncomfortable? Do you find it difficult to talk to your manager or does she find it difficult to talk to you? Do you find that when you do talk, there's a lot of miscommunications? If you don't get along with your boss, it's a miserable experience. You don't need to be best friends, but you do need to establish a mutually acceptable working relationship. By using the suggestions you'll find on how to manage your boss, the relationship should benefit greatly.

Helping you help your boss be more effective. Many direct reports know what their boss is doing wrong but don't know how to communicate it without negative repercussions. Or they have ideas they believe would help their boss run the group even more effectively than he does, but they are uncertain about how to propose these ideas without causing their boss to respond defensively or angrily. Another benefit of this book is that it will give you tactics to make your boss a more effective manager and the group more productive.

Giving you tools to increase your work quality in the short term and boost your career in the long term. Knowing how to work with your boss with greater efficiency and effectiveness can result in many short-term gains—you'll receive more challenging assignments and ones that take better advantage of your talents. In the long run, your efforts will help your boss better appreciate your contributions and rely on them more. Your achievements will be noted by your manager (and by others in the organization), who should be favourably disposed to reward you with raises, promotions, and so on.

Be visible

If your superiors don't see you or know who you are, you're very easy to let go. Out of sight, out of mind, and—poof! —you're gone. Accentuating and improving your physical presence and raising your overall profile at work are, together, the first steps toward locking down your job security.

You need to do is to create a perception that makes you more visible, more notable, and ultimately more valuable to your company. That means, for example, that you don't actually have to pull all-nighters twice a week to show how committed you are to your job. You do need to arrive at work before your boss and leave after she does in order to create the impression that you're there all the time. And you need to go out of your way to meet and engage people—coworkers, managers, even the CEO—who will unwittingly become a part of a team of people who will help you bulletproof your job.

Make damn sure you're not invisible at the critical times when decisions are being made about who stays and who goes. Because the invisible guy is the first to go. 80 percent of success is showing up early. More to the bulletproof point, it's showing up earlier than your boss. The rest is a magical combination of talent, exceptional effort, and good luck. Arriving at work early shows your commitment and industriousness. Of course, you need to get there only five minutes before your boss or coworkers every day to come off as the world's most committed employee. Besides making it clear to your superiors that you take your job seriously enough to be more than on time, showing up early— before the phone starts ringing or your coworkers start bugging you—gives you valuable time to prepare for your day. Or rather, it gives you time to look as if you're prepared for your day. Sure, it's a bluff, but if you make it a habit, you'll always be ten steps ahead of the idiots who straggle in late all the time. The same goes for meetings or conference calls or any other appointments. Be there early to get your ducks in a row. Showing up late, looking unprepared or discombobulated, isn't quite the impression to cultivate if you want to keep your job. Bosses and coworkers hate when you show up late for meetings. Hate it. So, don't.

Stay later

Don't stay late, just stay later. Leaving a mere ten minutes after your boss has gone reinforces the impression that you're the world's most committed employee. It also shows that you're not a clock-watching nine-to-fiver.

Do step out of the office for lunch or even just a short walk to clear your head. Better yet, do it while your boss is at lunch, so she never sees you not working and never has to wonder where you are. But keep it to twenty minutes or less, unless you're having a business lunch, in which case make sure your boss knows where you are, and aim to keep it to an hour, ninety minutes tops.

Pay close attention to exactly what's going in the office when you make plans. Think about spacing out your vacation time in chunks of three or four days at a time instead of two weeks at once, so you're not out of the picture for too long a stretch.

Dealing The Boss Who Holds You Back

The Problem. You've been quietly showing your boss the ropes for a long time. He relies on you heavily for help with everything from interpreting monthly reports to sizing up market demand to placating cranky stakeholders. Yet only his name appears on the e-mails that update higher-ups on your projects. You feel like the stagehand behind the curtain—you're running the show, but he's the one out front, taking a prolonged bow.

Why It Happens? When the person who should be your organizational guide and cheerleader keeps your smart contributions under wraps, of course you don't feel valued. Even if he's not intentionally undermining you or holding you back, it's hard to stay motivated—after all, you know your efforts will go unrecognized. Some bosses simply don't like sharing the spotlight.

Others get nervous when their shortcomings are thrown into sharp relief by a direct report's strengths. You may run into this problem with a boss who is new to his job, for example, and feels threatened by your deep organizational knowledge and close internal ties. Or perhaps your manager inherited you in a merger or a reorg and has discovered that you bring critical new skills to his team—skills everyone assumed he already had.

What to Do About It? Jessica Pryce-Jones, of the leadership consultancy said people are often too quick to dub a work relationship a failure before taking their share of responsibility for fixing it. You may fantasize about changing jobs, but you probably won't have to resort to that. You can improve your day-to-day relationship with your manager—but you'll need to lead the transformation.

Remember that your boss wants to succeed in his job as much as you do in yours. That will help you adopt a constructive mind-set so that you can move beyond your frustration and improve the dynamic. Think about what you share with your boss rather than what divides you: If you have only "transactional" conversations, you're unlikely to warm to each other. But looking for personal similarities will make it easier for you to connect professionally.

Did you grow up in the same area? Do you admire the same people? Finding common ground will help you interpret events and interactions more positively. Are there reasonable explanations for what you perceive as negative signals? Maybe your boss appears to be shutting you out of critical meetings with his boss.

It's hard to strike a healthy balance with an alternately indifferent and needy boss who shuts you off from others. Haris was smart to put his name on his contributions and form alliances with other senior managers—otherwise, he'd have remained isolated and resentful—but it probably wasn't the best idea to go behind his paranoid boss's back (or over his head). That just fed the perception that he couldn't be trusted with independence and visibility.

Once you're open to his point of view, you can begin treating him as you'd like to be treated. Find genuine opportunities to make him look good. "*Tell someone he respects—perhaps one of his peers—about an insight he shared with you or something he accomplished that you admired,*" Pryce-Jones suggests. And express your appreciation after he helps you meet an important goal or solve a tough problem. You don't need to be effusive. Just sincerely acknowledge what he's done for you. At the very least, you'll lower his defences. Best case, you'll set a gracious example that he wants to follow. Tap his former direct reports. If you can easily get in touch with someone who used to work for your boss, invite her out for coffee.

Approach your boss in the most constructive way possible. Let him know that you're on his side. Say you want to find better ways to support him. No good will come of sulking with your arms folded or ranting about how unappreciated you are. Even if that's true, your boss won't respond calmly to that—he'll get defensive. After you've set a positive tone by putting his needs front and canter, make it clear that you're looking to grow, too. Explain that you're hoping to do that within the organization—ideally with his guidance. But say you'll also consider outside opportunities after a certain amount of time has passed (offer a reasonable time frame—maybe a year). To give him something concrete to work with, describe your big-picture professional goals and how you envision getting there. Suppose, for instance, you're eager to build your analytical skills: Volunteer to take on assignments that will require you to gather and interpret data. For example, you might comb through customer renewal rates to see if there are any patterns worth discussing. Ask your boss if he has other suggestions for developing those skills in your current role or if he'd recommend ways to get other senior managers in the company to see you in a new, high-potential light. Of course, once your cards are on the table, be prepared for things not to go your way. But at least you'll have given yourself and your boss every opportunity to right the course.

Ch7

Winning Office Politics

In a survey by the UK-based management-consulting firm Revelation, 95% of respondents said that manipulation and hidden agendas in the workplace had affected them personally. Maybe you're plagued by an office bully who constantly questions what you're doing and undermines you in meetings. Or a boss who pits you against your peers. Or a clique that wields an inordinate amount of organizational power. Perhaps you've even encountered backstabbing, one-upmanship, or shifting alliances.

Work is truly a critical component of happiness. Unlike the other creatures on the planet, people need to have a purpose. Those whose lives lack meaning feel lost and often drift into harmful, self-destructive activities. Unfortunately, if people lack clear goals, have unpleasant working relationships, or simply don't understand how organizations operate, the joy of accomplishment is often replaced by frustration and disappointment. When people fail to master the political side of work, their jobs may become unrewarding and unhealthy.

John was an extremely bright, capable executive with a clear and inspired vision for his organization. He had a true passion for his work and a great desire to do good things in the world. The problem, however, was that he had gotten completely sidetracked by his intense animosity toward his boss, embarking on an obsessive quest to get this man fired. Soon John started soon looking for another job.

Despite the diversity of settings in which one works, the same issues arise with remarkable consistency. Here are a few of the people that many encounter on a regular basis:

• A confused and anxious employee who is not sure exactly what is expected by management

• A tired and angry person who is clearly in the wrong job

• A frustrated manager who does not know how to deal with a poorly performing employee

• People at all levels who feel that their boss is incompetent, unfair, or unreasonable

• Colleagues who have constant disagreements because of drastically different work styles

• Entire departments at war with each other because of conflicting roles

• Many, many people who feel that they are somehow being treated unfairly

All these unhappy folks are, in one way or another, dealing with political dilemmas. When you view "office politics" not as a Machiavellian plot, but as a normal aspect of work that needs to be managed, you quickly realize that political ability is a fundamental component of success in any job.

When people are good at wining office politics, what are they able to do?" They able to:

Get their projects moved up the priority list

Play golf with important people
Influence management
Have their own office
Bypass normal procedures
Advance quickly
Get asked to solve the toughest problems
Receive more recognition
Accomplish results
Get things done despite great obstacles
Get senior management to "buy in" on projects
Help bring about changes
Get other people to do their work
Draw attention to a project
Get more money in their budget
Acquire resources for their staff
Stay out of trouble
Have their ideas heard
Get raises when other people don't
Survive changes

How to you win at politics?

Almost everybody does politics, but nobody is comfortable discussing exactly what they do. Many people feel that playing the political game involves devious plotting or blatant self-promotion. But in reality, "politics" is what naturally happens whenever people with different goals, interests, and personalities try to work together.

The political side of work quickly becomes apparent as soon as we take our first job. To succeed, we not only have to do outstanding work, but we also have to deal with quirky bosses and annoying co-workers.

Colleagues get defensive when we point out their mistakes, unscrupulous rivals try to stab us in the back, and managers make decisions that seem totally unfair—or completely idiotic. Learning to deal with these realities, and succeed in spite of them, constitutes our on-the-job political education. Every office is a playing field for the game of politics. And when you take a job, you're automatically a player.

Making yourself known in appropriate ways is simply smart—but talking about specific tactics can make people cringe a bit. Just as some have a natural aptitude for math, music, or golf, others seem to possess innate political talent. These instinctive abilities give them the same competitive advantage at work that natural athletes have in sports. But while you can improve your golf score by signing up for lessons, it's pretty tough to find tutoring in office politics.

Sharpening your political ability can increase the odds of accomplishing whatever objectives are important to you, but first you must clearly differentiate between goals and wishes. Wishes put the focus on what we want "them" to do. Goals give us power by describing results that we intend to accomplish. When converted to goals, the wishes see here would look like this:

This Political Golden Rule should be followed by anyone hoping to become a Winne. Never advance your own interests by harming the business or hurting other people.

Political Intelligence and the Facts of Life. The need for Political Intelligence is universal. Anyone, in any job, can use these skills to make work more productive and pleasant. To be a Winner at office politics, you must accept certain fundamental truths about the way organizations operate.

Winners often seem to have a "sixth sense" that helps them successfully navigate turbulent political waters. They get along with even the prickliest people and can bring up controversial issues without provoking or offending anyone.

Developing a high Political IQ can help you do many things:

- Clearly define the steps that will lead to our goals

- Recognize the power relationships in any group

- Capitalize on opportunities to increase your personal power and influence

- Identify the true motives and hidden agendas of others

- Remain focused on important objectives and ignore distractions

- Build positive relationships, even with unpleasant people

- Respond appropriately to both devious and direct attacks

- Turn conflicts and arguments into productive discussions

- Avoid wasting energy on irrelevant issues and unattainable goals

Mastering Political Skills. Researchers have identified four components of office political skill:

Astuteness:
This is the foundation of being a good office politician: being able to read others, your organisation and yourself. If you cannot interpret the signals of people around you, there's little likelihood of you working out how to get your way. If you do not understand how your organisation works, you will be blundering about in the dark. If you are not clear what you want, how are you going to act in ways that will get it? You must try to be as astute as possible about others, your organisation and yourself.

Effectiveness:
Having understood what is going on and made plans, you have to be skilled at executing them. That means knowing which combination of tactics to use, who to direct them at, choosing the right moment and performing the words and deeds effectively, always with some measure of actual thespianism – deliberate pretences and acting.

Networking:
Carefully nurtured relationships, within and beyond your organisation, enable you to press the right buttons. They build your reputation, oil wheels and are vital for moving between jobs.

The appearance of sincerity:
The closer the fit between who you really are and who you come across as, the better. But quite often, the inner and the outer must necessarily be different in

order for you to achieve successful management of the impression you are creating. You need to be able to do this in ways that seem sincere. If your colleagues have lost faith in your honesty and integrity, it will be hard to progress. If you can be more conscious of what you and others get up to, you will be much better able to do good for others, as well as yourself. Being shy or self-deceiving about this will only make you frustrated and resentful. You will be thwarted and outwitted by better operators. I am hoping to persuade you that there is nothing wrong with being a good office politician and improve your skills.

Symptoms of office politics to be ignnored

In office politics, here are some common themes you'll notice throughout:

1.Question your reaction: When people appear to be playing political games, we often think we know their motives, but sometimes we're off the mark.

2. Step back and reevaluate: What else could be driving the behaviour? Maybe it's not as vengeful as it seems—or even intentional.

3.Try removing yourself from the equation: Everybody brings her own quirks, worries, and stresses to work.

What you assume is a personal attack may have absolutely nothing to do with you.

4. Accept that not all conflict is bad: Great performance can come out of being challenged by an aggressive colleague or being forced to collaborate with someone who you can't stand. We can and often do rise to challenges. Don't assume "uncomfortable" means bad.

5.Take charge of your fate: Even if the playing field isn't level, you'll accomplish little by complaining about it. Assume responsibility for your progress. Don't give your manager and others any reason to dismiss you as a whiner.

6.Keep your cool: Office bullies and other game players win every time they see they have rattled you. Never give them that satisfaction—you'll just perpetuate the problem. Stay composed, and they'll lose their power.

Way to deal the Boss who adds problems

Here are ways to deal such bosses in different situations.

Situation: *Your boss has you competing against your peers for respect and attention.*

It's a "reindeer games" scenario—only one of you can win some coveted prize, whether it's the chance to lead a team, get a promotion, or just have a moment in the limelight. He or she has created a horrible, cutthroat environment for an otherwise collegial group of direct reports.

Why It Happens? Some bosses don't realize they're creating this problem, in many cases it's a deliberate management tactic. Task several people with solving a business challenge, and make it an implicit horse race. Even when a promotion isn't on the table, senior executives often leave roles and responsibilities ambiguous as a test. They want to see who can take the pressure, who will rise to the occasion, who wants to get ahead badly enough to throw some sharp elbows.

How to deal? You and your colleagues can find your own ways of working together that don't ratchet up the competition. Amelia figured this out early in her career, when an indifferent boss unwittingly set up a rivalry between Heath and a coworker. "We were in two different areas," She recalled, "but we needed to work together. Our boss didn't make roles and decision rights clear for us, so we had to sort them out ourselves." The colleague wanted to take the lead, just tapping Heath for whatever support he needed. But Amelia didn't intend to play a supporting role. In fact, her colleague relied on resources she controlled. Rather than engage in passive-aggressive games, Amelia decided to have a straightforward discussion with him about how they could work together on a level field. "It was a tough conversation," she recalls, "because we were held accountable for different things." They tried to keep emotion out of it by focusing on coming to an understanding that would benefit both of their teams. "We came up with a detailed plan for how we'd handle certain situations. And we agreed to not make any big commitments or moves without talking to each other first." It wasn't a perfect solution, but by dealing with the issue directly, they diffused what could have been an incendiary relationship. Susan an OD & HR expert suggested, what if your colleague is playing dirty—by one-upping you in meetings, for example, or leaving you out of the loop so that you'll look clueless? Describe exactly what you see him doing, and ask him to stop. You may not feel comfortable confronting him, but work up the courage to do it. He'll be more likely to play fair in the future because he probably doesn't enjoy confrontation any more than you do.

Situation: The control-freak boss

Your boss is smothering you. At first you thought, "It's because I'm new—that's why he insists on reviewing every document before I distribute it and sitting in on all my meetings." But now that you're no longer learning your role, the tight leash feels downright oppressive and embarrassing. The other day, he actually scolded you for having a hallway chat with one of his peers about an idea you've been kicking around. You're hardworking, competent, smart. How are you ever going to escape your boss's shadow?

Why it happens? Your boss is acting this way for a reason—though he may not be aware of it. Think about what could be driving his behaviour. His actions might be explained by factors that have little to do with you, such as a poor understanding of his role as manager, a micromanaging boss of his own, a lack of motivation to question how he's always done things, or personal insecurity.

What to do about it? "Few people get the guidance they need to become good managers. Accepting this may help you feel a little less frustrated with your boss. It's likely he's simply a flawed human being who thinks he is doing his best. Avoid his panic buttons. Form an educated guess about where your boss's sensitivities lie. If you believe, for example, that he's intimidated by those above him, think of ways you can alleviate that pressure, such as running reports to better prepare him for meetings with his manager. Or perhaps he's afraid that people don't perceive him as essential, and he's on a tear to prove how much you and others need him. Dispel his fears. Bring him any news you hear, and take your ideas to him before sharing them with others. As your boss begins to trust that you'll come to him without prompting, he may loosen his grip.

Don't fight it. Instead of viewing it as a blow to your ego think about how you might actually benefit from it. Your boss may have your best interests in mind. Perhaps he wants to ensure that you have a sound understanding of the company's proctor the most effective ways to work the system to get things done.

Regardless of the cause, accept that your boss may have something important to teach you. If your boss doesn't appear to have faith in your ability to do your job, consider whether you've given him a reason to feel this way. Have you missed important deadlines? Delivered presentations that fell flat? Assembled proposals that failed to win business? Take a hard look at yourself—and look around. If your boss isn't micromanaging other colleagues, his behaviour could be a clue that you're underperforming.

If you suspect that's the case, ask him about it, says Clark. Tell him you feel he's monitoring you extra closely and you want to understand what's behind it. Is there a particular area where he feels you need guidance? Some bosses are reluctant to be straight with employees about their shortcomings, especially if criticism might be met with hostility. They may go to extremes, such as overly aggressive monitoring, to avoid having awkward conversations. So, make it easier for your boss. Say you're genuinely interested in feedback on your weaknesses, even if it's hard to hear. Stay calm as you listen to the feedback (don't even let a grimace cross your face). Once you get a clear sense of where you stand, you'll have a better shot at addressing his concerns. Thank your boss for his insights and tell him that you want to come back to him with an improvement plan. You might need to soothe your ego for a day or two, but the sooner you return him with a proposal, the more seriously he'll take you. Ask if he can recommend potential mentors (inside or outside the company). demonstrate that. Emphasize how important his feedback is to your growth.

Develop other champions. If your boss is micromanaging you, others may notice and start questioning your skills. That's why it's critical to build relationships outside his ken. "It's so important not to have all your eggs in one basket. Have points of contact with other people who can see your good work," says leadership expert Herminia Ibarra.

Join interdepartmental committees, and get involved in cross-disciplinary pursuits. Tell him what you'd like to do before you volunteer so that you don't take him by surprise and trigger his instinct to micromanage.

The Boss's Pet. Your boss has a pet employee who gets the most interesting assignments and special perks, such as flexitime and an expense account. It drives you crazy.

Sometimes favouritism is actually fair. The pet has a burning talent and desire to excel, works hard without complaining, and shares the boss's goals and vision. Understandably, the boss is high on her star performer.

But what if she favours an average performer? In that case, her pet is just a buddy. Like everyone else, your boss enjoys having friends at work. So she may latch on to an employee she sees as a kindred spirit—someone with whom she's comfortable. Or perhaps she's inherited a direct report.

Stop obsessing. There's little point to moaning that your boss has a favourite and it's not fair. That's not going to change the situation. In fact, it could make things worse.

Communication and branding expert Dorie Clark says not to lose sight of decorum—especially when connecting through social media. If you (or your friends) post with abandon on Facebook, think twice about "friending" your boss. You can follow him or her on Twitter (or suggest that she follow you, if you're a prolific tweeter) as long as you keep it professional

Women employees want their performance to speak for itself. If I do good work, they think, it will be noticed—people will consider me for great assignments because I'm so productive and reliable. Unfortunately, that's not how it works. If you want to be top of mind, you need to boost your visibility. When you attend a conference, for example, send your boss a list of 10 takeaways you'd like to share with the team when you return. You'll impress boss with your initiative and team focus.

The disaffected boss. He's there physically but not in spirit. He doesn't meet regularly with your group or bother to fill any of you in on the critical decisions that senior management is wrestling with. So, you're often the last ones to hear about big initiatives and changes. Some bosses become so consumed with lining up the Next Big Thing on their impressive rise to the top that they lose interest in their present roles. Whatever the reason, it's probably not about you. It's all about him. When your boss lacks drive and commitment, it can be hard to see the upside. But you may actually benefit from his disinterest. It gives you a chance to fill the void with your own good work. If he doesn't seem to care about much of anything, then he's not likely to mind if you find ways to step in and raise your own profile, as long as your efforts don't make more work for him.

Ch8

Why You Didn't Get That Promotion

You've been passed over for a key promotion despite stellar results and glowing reviews. You've asked where you're falling short, but the responses have been vague and unsatisfying, leaving you angry, frustrated, and unsure of how to get ahead. Promotion decisions seem arbitrary and political. What's going on?

In most organizations, promotions are governed by unwritten rules—the often fuzzy, intuitive, and poorly expressed feelings of senior executives regarding individuals' ability to succeed in C-suite positions. As an aspiring executive, you might not know those rules, much less the specific skills you need to develop or demonstrate to follow them. The bottom line: You're left to your own devices in interpreting feedback and finding a way to achieve your career goals.

That's what happened to Harold Simson. He wasn't blindsided by the announcement that Nicole Bennett had been promoted to senior vice president and general manager for corporate markets. But Harold had been a contender, and this was the second time in four years he'd missed out on a division GM job. The first time, firm had hired an outsider who later left the position for a major role at a rival firm.

Harold always had excellent performance reviews. His 360 results indicated that people loved working for him, and as far as he could tell, managers across the company were beating down the doors to join his group. In terms of execution, his track record was flawless: He and his team had met or surpassed their numbers in each of the past five years. Additionally, they had successfully implemented every major corporate program during that time, and his division had recently been selected to serve as the pilot site for an SAP installation. When he'd learned of these last two GM assignments, he'd also been told that he had a great future with the company and that with a little "seasoning," he'd be ready for advancement.

To Harold, the promotion wasn't much of an expression of the company's leadership competency model, posted on his office wall. Harold bore Nicole no ill will, but it looked as though it was time to update his résumé and rekindle some relationships in his network. Distasteful as it was, testing the job market seemed to be the only way to advance.

Harold's situation is surprisingly common, especially among people the criteria for advancement. Though he had been considered for the GM role both times, in each instance there were bona fide concerns about his readiness.

However, his communication skills actually alluded to tensions with peers in other units. He could be overly competitive and slow to resolve conflict, whereas

Nicole's powers of persuasion allowed her to manage discord and achieve superior results. She was also known for developing talent. Working for her was not for the faint of heart, but she challenged her staff members, and they grew in the process. Ralph didn't recognize that his popularity reflected, in part, his reputation for being a little easy on people—he didn't stretch them to grow and develop. Managers flocking to his unit were often B players who knew he'd cut them some slack. He was luring talent that was good but not great; Nicole was attracting A players who wanted a push.

Harold was a go-to guy for implementing corporate initiatives, a master of continuous improvement. But senior management had seen no evidence of his ability to conceive a large-scale change that would produce a quantum leap in performance. Can strategic thinking be developed? That's open to debate, but the fact was that Harold had always worked for visionaries who never gave him the chance to flex his own strategic muscles, a problem everyone had overlooked.

In fact, at most companies, cohesion tends to fall short at senior levels thanks to rivalry and ego, but teams function pretty well nonetheless. Acquiring and developing talent is the executive's imperative, and teamwork becomes a nice-to-have. Harold's ability to orchestrate well-functioning teams to complete complex projects, among other skills, had singled him out for previous promotions. But when he was being considered for the GM jobs, strategic thinking became a much higher priority.

One obvious way to get insight is to approach your boss and colleagues directly for their opinions, though their input might be of limited use. They may not be straight with you, and their perspectives may differ from those of the most senior decision makers. For additional information, you might have a conversation with your former manager or your boss's boss. Try to contact the highest-level manager who is knowledgeable about your work and with whom you have a positive relationship, so your approach seems natural and appropriate. Caution, don't go behind your boss's back. He or she should know about any contact with other executives and what your intentions are.

Getting past executives' reluctance to provide direct and difficult feedback is tricky. When asking for input, project a sincere desire to understand what's holding you back—and avoid appearing to lobby or argue. Your core question should be "What skills and capabilities do I need to demonstrate in order to be a strong candidate for higher levels of responsibility at some point in the future?"

Get into active-listening mode. Any comment or body language that conveys defensiveness will most likely cause the other person to either clam up or move the conversation to easier (and vaguer) territory—such as the need for more "seasoning" that Harold kept hearing about. Ask clarifying questions, but don't challenge the content. Be alert to code words and phrases masking fundamental issues—general observations about the need for "increased leadership ability" or "better teamwork" or "improved communication."

Juliana Bryant needed to improve her leadership skills before she'd be eligible for her next promotion. She was managing multiple initiatives, and her teams were functioning effectively; she didn't see how to improve her leadership except by taking on more projects. She discovered that in her dedication she in fact had been doing herself a disservice. She'd been given an ever-increasing number of projects because of her superior organizational and people-management skills and her ability to stay on top of details. However, senior managers were concerned that she was maxed out by her personal involvement in every initiative and wanted to see that she could delegate more and create processes and systems that would ensure flawless execution without so much direct supervision.

Changing deep-seated perceptions of you takes visible and consistent effort. In response Juliana put considerable effort into rethinking how she spent her time: which issues she should be involved in personally, which she could—with some coaching—learn to delegate to others, and what kinds of meetings and reports would allow her to stay as close to projects as was needed. A year later she was promoted to lead a large operational unit.

Things don't always work out so well. If you are having trouble decoding the feedback you receive, try asking at the end of each session, "What one or two things—above all others—would most build confidence in my ability to succeed at higher levels within the organization?" As long as the other person answers honestly, this question tends to circumvent vagueness and separate the wheat from the chaff. Keep in mind that changing deep-seated perceptions about you, formed over years, requires visible and consistent effort—which is why it is typically best to focus on one or two key areas of development.

If you're serious about landing a promotion, there are a few things that need to happen first.

Get clear expectations from your boss. Make the boss happy. Sit down with your manager and set specific goals for yourself. "Say, 'I want to hit the ground running and exceed your expectations. What can I do?'" recommends Julie Cohen, career coach. Express that you'd like to connect quarterly to review your performance, says Cohen, and use your first meeting to broach the subject (e.g., "*As you can see, I'm committed to delivering great work. What will it take to get promoted?*")

Document your achievements. Your boss probably isn't tracking your every accomplishment, so keep a log of your quantifiable accomplishments—that way you have concrete results to cite when you ask for a promotion. It's the "strategic bragging." Also, record the skills you acquire and make sure to consistently update your resume to reflect them.

Cozy up to HR. A friend in HR may be your ticket to nabbing a promotion. Take the person to lunch to start building rapport. Once you've established a relationship, your confidant may even be able to tip you off about promotion opportunities in other departments. HR has a pulse on what's happening across the organization.

Push beyond your job description. Once you've proven yourself capable of delivering great work, ask your manager to take on more responsibility. But be specific by asking to work on particular tasks or projects. You want to take on "stretch assignments," or jobs that give you a trial run at the promotion you're eyeing. You can say, "I heard there's going to be a new product line. How can I get involved with that?" Requesting specific work also shows initiative. "Don't put the onus on your boss to find you new responsibilities."

Prove you're a leader. While your boss wants to see you're a team player, you still need to distinguish yourself from your peers. "Individuals get promoted, not teams," says Asher. Executive coach Joel Garfinkle, author of Getting Ahead: Three Steps to Take Your Career to the Next Level advises taking ownership of a group project. "Even if there's not an assigned leader, assume that role," he says. "Be the one who makes the final presentation. Be the one who updates the boss."

Ask for the promotion. It sounds basic, but many employees expect their boss to hand them a promotion. However, if you don't ask, you shall not receive.Of course, there's the possibility that you won't get promoted (even if you do all of the above). There may be circumstances outside your control. The company could freeze raises, your boss quits, or— gasp! —one of your peers gets tapped for the job. If it's the latter, find out why you were passed over, but keep the focus on you. Say, "What could I have done differently so that would have been me?" Then, use the feedback to improve your performance and position yourself for a promotion in the coming year.

Find that promotion somewhere else. If you've been killing it at work, but there's still no pay raise or title change in sight, you might have to cut your losses. Many times, actually more often than not, a promotion is easier to attain at a new job than at your current employer. And making a move could bring more than a salary bump. There's often a signing bonus, new title, more responsibility and leadership roles that come with a promotion. So, keep proving yourself to your boss, but if you feel stuck for too long, it might be time to re-vamp your resume and start looking for a new job.